W9-CXZ-486

BOY AT THE SCREEN DOOR

Poetry by
BRUCE SPANG

Cover and book design by Nancy Bush,
Violette Graphics & Printing

Copyright © 2014 Bruce Spang
All rights reserved.

ISBN 978-1-4675-7262-0

Published by Moon Pie Press, Westbrook, Maine
Please visit our website at www.moonpiepress.com

Dedication

My partner, Myles Rightmire, for his love and support

811
Spa

2016/05 g

Cover Photograph:

From David Hilliard's book *David Hilliard Photographs*. New York: Aperture, 2005, "Norm's Birthday, 2001." David has a new book called *What Could Be*. Seattle: Minor Matter Press, 2014.

Hilliard's gentle diptychs and triptychs conjure a world that begins with the visual but extends far beyond it to the narrative. He chooses to see, and to create, beauty in the narratives he imagines for himself, his friends, and striking strangers he encounters. Some of his subjects are frosted with perfect light and rich, dripping colors redolent of the peak of summer; others are subdued, bearing an uncertainty and fragility that so often accompanies the process of self-awareness. His images ask that the observer cease to be an observer, but rather enter into the way one image contains a narrative, filled with paradox and yearning, enchantment and loving. He makes you see the world differently. His images evoke the dream stories of our lives.

Acknowledgments:

Thanks to Betsy Sholl, Gil Helmick, Melissa Crow, Rachel Contreni Flynn, and Alice Persons for combing through these poems and teasing out the knots.

Off the Coast: "love song without birds and flowers"
                "In Our Room by the River"
The Aurorean:
                "The Drift"
Locuspoint: "York Beach, Now and Then"
                "Nate Writing His Own Short Story"
                "Where Few Voices Can Reach"
                "The Wrong"
                "Questions Midway Through a Reading by
                  Mary Oliver at Smith College"
Port City Poems (Maine Poetry Central, 2013):
                "Portland"
                "Coffee by Design"
Passion and Pride: Poets in Support of Equality (Moon Pie Press, 2012)
                "When"

OTHER POETRY BOOKS by Bruce Spang:

The Knot (Snowdrift Press, 2006)

To The Promised Land Grocery (Moon Pie Press, 2008)

I Have Walked Through Many Lives: Young Voices, Scarborough (Moon Pie Press, 2009) (editor)

Passion and Pride: Poets In Support of Equality (Moon Pie Press, 2012) (editor)

CONTENTS

III.

IV.

V.

Foreword:

Several years ago The Maine Humanities Council asked me to write about my becoming a poet. Many people responded positively to the article, so I include it as part of this book because it reflects how many of us as poets have learned our craft.

Coming to language was not easy for me. The written word eluded me during most of elementary school. I took third grade twice since my teacher discovered that I read from right to left, not left to right. Breaking words into syllables seemed by then, and is still now, an impossible task, so I memorized whole words, looking them up so I knew them on sight like an old friend. I was dyslexic before there was a term for it. Back then, I was labeled "slow" and worse, "dumb" because I could not figure out how words worked. I struggled mightily. But I did love words. They seem filled with mystery—like little surprises in a box of Cracker Jacks.

As a young writer, I had as much difficulty putting my words down on the page as I did in reading them. In English, I was a low C student. But in my sophomore year in high school, a teacher—her name was Mrs. English, oddly enough—found that I had something to say and encouraged me to write. Forget the grammar, forget the spelling (both were atrocious), just write—and I did. Later in college I kept a journal about my trip around Europe with my brother. He noted that I wrote like a poet; I used images and narratives with unexpected turns in them.

I knew nothing about poetry, so I took several courses in it to see what poets did. As with most poetry classes, the focus was on what poems meant, and I was bored until one day a real poet came to class. He talked about the language, the twists and turns in a poem and the way a poem has many meanings and different layers. I started taking my journal entries and shaping them into a poetic form. Some people liked them and asked me to read them more of my poems.

I was hooked. I liked how, if I worked on it, a poem could encapsulate an experience, could traverse the landscape of my feelings and thought, going from the highs to lows, in a short compact form. It was a tiny epiphany, a way of seeing experience through a new lens.

For much of my life, I worked alone, writing in journals, not showing my work to anyone. In my late thirties, I sought out several mentors who taught me how to craft my poems. In my late forties, I enrolled in the Vermont College MFA program. I learned the value of others giving me criticism. I completed the program with a new perspective on what is takes to write a good poem.

I still workshop my poems with a group of poets that meets once a month, because there is no end to what you can learn and how you can get the better of words. I keep reading and discovering new ways of saying things and reviving my life and my vision of life.

Throughout my life and the various occupations that I have been in — the ministry, counseling, drug and alcohol education, alternative education, school administration and teaching — poetry remained my one true avocation, something that took all the disparate parts of my life and brought them together.

Because poetry wants to find the wholeness in our fragmented world, because poetry wants to lead us out of the confusion into understanding, because is more interested in delight than resolution, I find it a source of endless hope and inspiration and, really, faith.

When the little inarticulate boy in me looks out on this vast world and witnesses the cruel and dreadful events that assault us daily, he wants to find wonder and often will turn to those mysterious words he found so hard to master. They console him and bring him back to trust and create a better vision of this world. As a teacher, when I see how language can transform lives — and how it does the same for me — I know that poetry can take any child who feels unheard and alone and put magic back into his or her life, filling it with meaning.

Poets speak not just to their own struggles but to us all. As long as there is poetry, then we shall in some ways — all of us — be heard. Poetry is its own democracy, a country that has no divisions, no boundaries, that reaches across time and across culture and language, to each of us and demands that each of our voices be heard.

January 2014

York Beach, Then and Again

I

Across the bay, the lighthouse licked the sky —
thirty years ago. My wife and I rented a cabin
on a cliff's edge, 100 feet over
rocks. The sea was not rumbling
a rhapsody, yet beckoned me to what?
To wanting other than a wife
beside me? Yet I rose each night
to her wanting and she, surprised
at my need — the lust, waves of it,
cried *oh* and *oh* and never
heard below, not me —
but the sea, coming
in, lifted. Never swerving,
we — she and I — let it take us
like an almost happiness.

II

There's no horizon, merely fog
and, below it, gray unveilings, a slither
of white lips paring the vast indifference
of gray. I'm waiting for someone
who's late, again. And yet, out of this shushing
of rocks and water in the mist-mothered air,
first one, then two, headlights blink by —
not my friend — but someone hurried.
It's nearly dinner time, the nightly news
blathers in some living room like a gull and
offshore — can't make it out —
keening like a door on worn-out, rusty hinges
the dark lick of lament over the murmurings of musts
and maybes and might-have-beens.
Then, nothing but gray.

I.

Before Dawn

The pale moonlight sprawls out
little by little like kindness on the floor.

And, yes, I weep because I want to slip beneath it,
have it hold me, until I sleep to the blessed hour

when frost still whitens even the darkest door
and no crows cackle on the leafless limbs,

when, in its solitary hour, goldfish idle in the tank
and guppies flit like thoughts from side to side.

Midnight dismembers me. I wake
from a dream of nails ripping at my eyes

and knives carving inside my mouth. I
stagger half asleep in the dark to the room,

that, by day, is bathed in light, but, now, is
dark and dense as death. On the floor

moonlight, limpid, lovely, breathlessly still
as a lover, undresses itself for me.

The Wrong

Press your fingertips to your wrist—
the bone, the nerves, the pulse—and, yes,
the skin, that delicate wrapping
like the skin of lilies,
their bright yellow mouths.

He slipped out his belt
and slapped it in his hand,
"Take that," and I did—
then fled to the garden.

The bee's rump nestled inside
the pliant folds of foxglove,
inside the violet blues of lupines,
consoling color inside of color,
flesh of hide, flesh of mine.

Sweet William, deep purples and whites,
the startling red of Iron Cross—these
kind colors, corpulent, glistening,
tender in the early light,
skin of my childhood, skin of my kin.

Where Few Voices Can Reach

These days I want someone to teach me to pray,
pray like the black lady, seated next to me
in her blue uniform, her fingers on her rosary,
bowing her head —
it's nearly midnight — our bus rumbles
toward 77th Street North,
where her free hand will pull the cord,
and a programmed voice will intone, *Stop Requested*,
to drop her off on some silent street
to be done with day.

I want someone to teach me to count beads,
psalm by psalm, into my heart's core as if I were back
on the freedom ride to Mississippi in 1969,
singing, *We are not afraid, blacks and whites together*,
my friend Reg, his skin sticky, hot next to me,
riding into a segregated south. We carried signs,
"Freedom Now," from Nashville, riding clear
across one state into another, eight long hours
to march by men in open convertibles, cradling
shotguns in their laps, confederate flags
on their t-shirts, scowling at us as we sang
every mile on the way, *we shall overcome*.

Now I'm the only white man taking the northbound
bus from the Center for the Performing Arts
where, not an hour ago, I was about to leave
the top tier of the concert hall when a gay man,
dragging his lame leg behind him,
stepped out from his chorus,
into center stage — alone at a microphone.

I wanted to turn my back on him, but he stood
there looking right up at me in the last row
in the dark recess of space.

I looked at the faces of men around me,
faces of any man — a banker before he denies
a loan, a lover before he turns away, an atheist
before he spits in God's eye — all staring at center stage.

The singer straightened up, opened his mouth.

His voice rose as if climbing one steep step at a time,
until the sound rose to where I stood — fourth tier —
then it peaked, soared and filled the concert hall.

Because he was singing about *the road to freedom*,
about *never turning back, how he lived and loved*
this life the best that he could and he could *finally fly*,
my body, tired and transfixed, filled with his sound.

Halfway to my destination — 110th Street North —
People the color of night hopping on, scrunched up,
people worn out with struggle, I'm still hearing his voice
and want to sing, *Ain't gonna let nobody turn me 'round*,
sing, *How we were gonna keep on walkin'*,
along with him, as if he were beside me,
as if there is still a prayer of hope
in this city of greed, in the heat of July,
on this bus as segregated at this hour
of the night in 2008 as in Montgomery in 1956.

Who can bother to pray any more?
Those voices who could pray
in those dreadful days decades ago —
all silenced. Where can I turn?
To a book I hold in my lap?
It's a *New York Times* bestseller
about how music fires neurons like passion,
arouses them to transport us with its pitch
and volume from one side of the brain to the other.

I remember my high school buddy, Reg,
back in 1965, crossing the Edmund Pettus Bridge,
marching to Selma, telling me how
the dogs and batons beat him back.
The song kept on moving.
It reached out past the growls and screams

just as that man's voice on the stage today
reached to where I was, tired
of listening to chorus after chorus,
ready to walk out that door.

I should have known what freedom songs can do—
I've heard them my whole life. It's just that
they are songs we sang long ago
when we believed that freedom *was* coming.
It's like a stop we never arrived
on this long ride into the night—
always another cord you have to pull first,
always the yet-to-be, a note you can't quite reach,
a song long forgotten.

But that lone singer's voice comes back to me,
perfectly pitched, his arms extending, reaching,
standing as tall as any man can stand,
joined by the men behind him;
men who believed, backed him up,
and his voice swept note by note into me
like something I'd forgotten—
like a prayer, and as the crowd rose
in a standing ovation, I stood
and watched him, his delicate hands
pressed together, held up in front of him,
bow as he blessed us all.

Salvation

There it was, the blue lid and yellow-green
jar sitting right on Greg's dresser — blatant —
as if announcing, "Come on let's do it."

He showed me how with just two fingers full
you could anoint yourself and rub, fast or slow,
the green oozing though your cupped hand, so that

practically all night, as you did with him,
you felt some kindred ecstasy, some sense
you arrived at glory singing *Ahh, AhhAhhh*

and remembered, how, when you were an infant,
your mother soothed your bottom and
you first knew what *Ahh* meant

and, later, after allergies encamped
in your sinuses and your nose, worn out,
with no end of *achoos,*

Vaseline came to your rescue.
No wonder Greg felt so at home with it.
Like evangelists converting believers,

down on the floor, legs extended, fists
full of praise, our eyes rolled back
knowing if there is a god he'd love

Vaseline. He'd join Greg and every
15-year-old, singing its praises, giving himself to it,
never wanting it to end. *So now at 68,*

as I open the medicine cabinet
and see the rectangular jar and the green *ohh,*
any wonder I want to slip my two fingers into it,

give myself over to it as someone
who's found Jesus, someone who believes
because he knows that Greg is standing

at his cabinet — he's retired and alone
in some condo in Orlando — and he
remembers too and reaches for it

and soon he's 15 and he smiles
at me and I smile back at him because,
hey, the lid flips open with one flick

of the thumb like he showed me. There is
no telling if we'll be this young — or this
happy — again, but, if there is salvation

(even in a jar), I'll take it any way I can.

The Drift

Snow remembers my tongue—
       how it tickles the tip,
       the tiny taste of time;
    remembers my feet—
       how the overshoes plop
       up and down in giant tracks;
    remembers my body—
       how it gives way like a lover,
       lets me sink into its sighs;
    remembers my longing—
       how I swoon into no-school day,
        the sifting flecks over my snowsuit;
    remembers my face—
       how it licks my cheeks with tears
       that trickle over them;
    remembers my hand—
       how I scoop it up, roll it, shape it
       into castles I enter like a king;
    remembers me—
       how I want to strip off these pressed pants,
       this tie, this starched shirt and step out of
remembering
       into the drift sweeping across the yard.

Knowing the Lines

I've always colored within the lines,
traced inside the triceratops,
so that giant ferns do not bleed
into its three blue horns,
into its red eyes,
and in back of him,
the black palms and sky, extinct.

By third grade I stayed in line for lunch,
waited my turn to misspell a word.

Lines were everywhere: in the snow
where dogs peed; in hallways
for the polio vaccine; on calendars
between Monday and Tuesday, dividing
May from June; in pre-game warm-ups
at the Biester gym, hundreds of fans lining bleachers;
in algebra, two columns of numbers
above the line in my desperate search for x.

The long line that wove
around Spring and Main Street
to see *Dr. Strangelove.* The line
Ralph gave Lidster about being in love,
and the graduation night line
where we put one foot in front of another —
a diploma, a cheer, a tossed cap —
and dismissed into a quiet diaspora.

The line we gave to the Selective Service
about being a conscientious objector,
Duffy already in a body bag
lined up on the tarmac in Saigon.

The line we signed on our marriage certificate.
And the one to annul it. The line about being only 48
when the lines in our faces exceed 68.

The line my brother gave about his white count,
and my mother about her being all right
when she'd fallen three times.

Lines keep getting longer
at gas pumps, on Black Friday,
at unemployment offices,
in soup kitchens, on election day

because of the lines about cutting taxes,
about prosperity around the corner,
about tomorrow and tomorrow and tomorrow.

Who else is standing in line?
Our sister at the oncology lab?
Our mother at another funeral parlor?
Our son on the expressway to nowhere?

What are we waiting for? For someone
to give us a crayon to color it right?
Color it so there's no mistake.
Color everyone, as McCarthy did,
color them all, red, red, red.

Or color them dead
like the lines at Treblinka
at the train depot, its clock
whose hands pointed to no-time-left,
by the lovely hedges and newly planted flowers
along the narrow path to the showers
where guards sang lines from the camp song?

Before Light

My brother and I haven't woken.
Over us, thin sheets dream on our skin.

The lake is the underside of a mirror;
Father and Mr. Grant, so far out
in the darkness, trolling
in their motorboat before dawn,
cannot be seen from the dock.

Not then, not later.
Dark and adrift.
                    Fishing.
Smudges on the horizon.

When they arrive back,
bright trophies of fish pulse on the dock.

We stroke and smooth their scales
until a light from within them reveals
red, silver blue and the yellow dawn
they were dragged into.

Years before, Mr. Grant caught us
tumbling in open bags of lime
looking like Hopi deities.

"For God's sake, don't touch your eyes."

He grabbed us, stripped off our clothes.
We pranced under pressure of the hose.

He lathered us. By the fury of his mighty
worried hands, he rubbed our bright burning
skin as if scaling us, scraping us clean,
wrapped and white as filets Father loves to fry.

The Osprey

for George VanDeventer

skims across sky, above pines
        lake
peering   into shallows,
(pulse   air under wings)
catches a glint of fin,
hovers, adjusts,
plunges
lift   gone —
wings ripped back
plummeting
eyes invisible blue
calculating, adjusting,
focus   there
the image   water —
drawing in his wings —
this is   falling freely —
a tuck   a dive
before smacking
        slapping back
    wings,
thrust talons into water,
plunge, immerse,
          contact
food for belly,
a prize   a love —
water grips him,

wet, awkward, his wings
      drag   weight,
flutter,
      great thrust of muscle,
shake   off
adjust to squirming life —
          wants no part of him —
    yet   turns to face forward,
the bright shining   he can taste
    he will not to let go: he wants
       to
          live.

In Our Room by the River

for Sally Dobres

Lumps of snow from the sycamore
thump on the porch. We open our eyes.

Light fingers up white sheets.
Our different sexes bathe in light.

You slid over me. March ice
masks the Potomac. Now it cracks.

White traffic jams its banks.
Ice boulders shove on shore.

Giant crystals glisten in light.
Our bodies press still and close.

The river rises with run-off and sweeps
the ice away. We shiver at the sight.

We no longer live in that room. We're far
from the river. Far from that shore.

Some mornings in these older years
when light slips in the window

faintly, yet surely, I hear
snow drip slowly off the sycamore.

Three Watercolors by Charles Demuth

In 1917 when he was 34,
Demuth painted men in a Turkish bath,
dressing, disrobing—naked,
men with muscular bodies—
awash in cadmium yellow,
their eyes riveted on one another.
Gallery owners refused to show them.
He kept painting—a self-portrait,
his pencil-thin mustache, his naked body
pressed against another man;
poppies with muscular petals;
red zinnias in a vase nestled
next to two lemons;
paintings stroked by the same hand—
towering factories and smokestacks
against an ultramarine sky—
dabbed with subtle colors.
He painted and painted.

It's 2010 and I'm 64—standing
in the museum alcove,
enraptured with his watercolors,
what he dared to see as beautiful
in the dim light of the baths: a man
looking at another man
                              with love.

Adieux

I crate the tomatoes, wrap each in old news,
set several on the sill to ripen,
bid adieu to those tart remnants on my tongue.

There's Mary Travers on the radio, gone —
slicing with the smoky resonance of her voice
a C-sharp like she's here, reincarnate.

There's word of Teddy, dead, no longer
catching his breath as if he could retrieve
Mary Jo from his drowned Oldsmobile.

In photographs of them, they're old and frail,
waving at a camera already turned. Just outside
the window, a calendula, button-faced, yellow,

a late-comer, stands sturdy on its long stem.
I slop mayonnaise on a tomato and savor
its wet, acid imprint, ruddy, torn out of time.

love song without birds and flowers

you and who he was were lasting
in the whisper of the willing now,
turning of one body to another,
not asking if or why but touching—
Oh my and the kindred ecstasy
that rises only and needs no name;
it's fine because fire never asks who
it consumes: it takes absolutely you;
so don't ask *if* and *can it be*:
it does as it will do—
O body, let love be *Yes*—
it wants you to curl up
next to next as someone in no need
of metaphor because he is what is
and takes and gives what is given
and sleeps in the comfort of
Yes, it's so and let it go

Before Stonewall

Richard called me —
he'd fallen — he's seventy.

On his boots, no grips, he slid —
Thunk — his rump witless kissed

and *thwack* his head smacked curbstone
out like the night the chaperone

flicked off the lights, seventh grade,
everyone nuzzled up, horny to be laid.

No one knew who was who, but Dave
sidled hip to hip, his hand engraved

with thirteen-year-old lust and lips
to lips kissed *me*, whispered shush.

I felt as if I slipped on ice
because he kissed me twice.

I fell in love with what Love was —
unmasked desire that fled because

the light came on, as it did for Richard,
concussed, light years away, word-

less. There he was. Someone beheld him
or what, sprawled out, he had been

just as I beheld Dave, his hand in Pattie's
winking at me, impish, pleased.

Bright Ambition of the Wind

From the doorstep as far as far can go,
hoarfrost coats hollyhock and hibiscus,
a scrim over the green of everything,
a pale lament moaning,

Enough, enough, be still. Roots numb.
Chalky green crumbles to coffin-brown
across the yard into what seems like
infinity. Mowers quiet. Wild grasses strut

late summer on strong stems, but bow
like courtiers to the Queen of November.
She shudders, *No, not now,* and sweeps
with a flick of her fist her white gown down.

None defy her, none breathe a word.
Even five upstart calendula yelling, *Yellow, yellow*
and eight—count them—eight fresh raspberries,
she passes by, freeze. Yet rebellion stirs.

Even now: Narcissus, self-absorbed,
tease soil with their roots, *Just wait, just wait.*
She'll have none of it. White reigns,
night gags days, nothings left, nothing.

An old cat curls by a window.
Light curtsies, submits. *It's done.* It slips away . . . .
In five months, six, morning will tap on the pane,
It's time. It's time. All is not as it seems.

In between the was and will be, the counting hours
within fisted gloves, below the massive troops
of cold, over sunflowers bent and broken,
the Queen promenades on what has been,

sure she's queen, ubiquitous, in charge—
her likenesses on every snow-walled street,
at every corner. Stern palace guards
defend her heart of ice, her every move.

Quiet. She reigns. Let her be.
Quiet. Wait while waiting is wise.

II.

How Earth Awakens

— a prayer for my brother

How gently light falls on the nubs
of snowdrops, crocus and jonquil buds.
Ever the cool crisp air of morning
coming on, ever a light remembered

on the hill in Norway: the bleats
of sheep outside our tent, the deep
fjords with ice in their crystal veins
and raspberries, ripe, and the remains

of summer in the high hill, one more
ferry across a jut of rock, one more door
to another land, so many borders crossed,
so many gates swung open and not lost

up a mountain pass, the white petals
like a wreath on your head, and the stem
in your mouth, traipsing down the fen
singing *how lovely, lovely the meadow.*

Standing at dawn at the Berlin Wall,
the binoculars of guards on the other side
eye you with your T-shirt waving "hi"
to those behind barbed wire seven feet tall,

the wall that failed to keep them from leaping
to freedom, crossing the gate to stand
in the brightness of the brittle morning
where going and coming can

be as easy as opening a flap of the tent
and seeing the mouths of lambs content
in green grass and there to stand upright
and yawn transfixed at the eternal light.

In the land of the midnight sun where
we sip coffee, cut a slab of fresh bread
and plot which road leads to Bergen
where pastries like jewels are fed

to raucous gulls. The enormous ferry
nuzzles against the aching pier. Up
the gangplank we trekked to the top
deck and to the coast slipping nearly

to a jagged line in our quicksilver
memory of standing on the hill crest
where day was night and night never
came, and, we, awakened, were blessed.

Questions Midway through a Mary Oliver Reading at Smith College

Do you linger on a line?
Dwell, wondering if it will end,
or start: a path along the comfrey,
bluebells soundless as you pass?

Does the languor of a line trouble you
as it ends, as if it could not bear another
breath, and there is nothing left to say?

Outside the hall, little exasperations
of asters claim some portion of the sun,
while students, unaware as yet of the angst
in the effort to arrange such colors to bloom
in a tight container, hurry past them to hear you.

They mouth whole stanzas you read
as if the lines were already their lines,
as if the grasshopper you held
in your hand they hold, as if the swan
that you admit was actually a goose
could swim away from their meanings .

How can they know how hard those asters,
cropped, planted — proper in their place —
work to be noticed on the steps that rise
to the oaken doors, to the crowded aisles,
to the podium and, lovely, to your feet
where they listen, rapt, as you speak?

Stuck

My grandson throws one,
another stick —
he has a good arm —
into the creek.

Some make it.
Some catch on rocks.

One stick shivers yet stays.

I supply him, as my son
before him, with sticks:

Go   Stop

Yes   No

What does he know?
He likes to throw.

This I Ching, my first lover told me,
I'll show you how it works.
He had me ask three sticks
two questions

Will our love last?
Does he love me as I love him?

then, pick out sticks

Yes   No

Later that night, folded
in his arms, he told me

No

My grandson tosses
sticks out

So many sticks.
        So many rocks.
                So little water.

Putting It On

A cool November night, we gather in the locker room,
boys in jeans, in shirts like drooping flags,
open our lockers and unbuckle our belts —
our thighs white as chickens — pull off our shirts,
tug on one leg, then another,
slip them off, Fruit of the Looms, a last reluctance to nakedness,
to our hopelessly adolescent bodies —
a few snatches of chest hair, concave chests,
blubbery bellies, shy belly buttons,
and two nipples like puckered pimples.
Down comes underwear, shriveled penises,
some short and slight as corks,
others thin as Oscar Meyer wieners, and hurriedly,
up comes jockstrap, cock in pouch, soft hideaway.
Two straps snuggle our rears.
We'd wiggle into t-shirts, slip on shoulder pads,
lace up, tighten down, shimmy into skin-tight pants
and wrestle down the jersey — numbered now: 32, 78
tuck it in, buckle pants. Shoes laced up, double knots;
cleats clicking on the cement. We pick up helmets and hold them
in our laps, our hands on plastic colored green and white.
We eye each other, wordless, waiting for the coach,
who struts in, hands on hips. "Ready, boys?" he says,
appraising us. We bow our heads. He offers a prayer,
and then, opens the door on the corridor. We step,
our cleats like little SOS's into the stadium — the roars,
the field, the lights — sprinting through goal posts,
helmets on, like almost gods.

The Ocean Takes Back Words That the Poet Took

You know who she is, the one with embroidered cowboy boots,
who drifts in and finds the sunniest spot,
lounges on her poncho and jots down her apercus,
grabbing words from me, words that spill out because
I can't help it—I make sounds—but she thinks it's me
speaking to her mythic mind and to her sisters of the surf,
as if she's a mermaid herself scribbling *ocean, ocean, ocean, ocean.*

Can she be with me as a lover after making love;
as a baker after the bread is fresh out of the oven;
as the moon after it presses its soft hand on my belly?
Shhh, put your notebook away; let's touch.
Sink your feet in sand; wiggle around, wait.
Yet, there she is, scribbling *ocean, ocean, ocean.*

I slam down waves like a straight flush.
That's the way I speak.
But she took *floor* and *shore* and *door* and *more*
as if I—and I alone—speak in monosyllables.
I'm polysyllabic. I want those words back.
Waves have seen her rush right up to them
and pluck *foam* off their neck.
Periwinkles complain. She's said they *roam*
in tidal pools. Look: they wince at her hair
flying everywhere. They dare not spell
words in their slime but recoil, silent in their shells.

My waves splatter against the granite
without expectation of applause or verse
praising their *plash* and *panache*. Explicitly
they say nothing but persist as they are,
being waves, each one rising up
and peaking over sand, against rock,
into crevasses and *plush*—
that's all they say—and, yes, *splash*
and *slush* and *kersplush* and thousands
more, depending on the shore. It's all in fun
(the sounds) and without intent to perform
for the lady with the pen and poncho.

She claims they pursue a higher aim,
to patter in iambic pentameter that she
alone, standing there, with her hip-length
hair, can hear — *ocean, ocean, ocean, ocean* . . . .

Does she pay attention to how many waves descant
to the shore and withdraw in a breath?
Does the clarinet want her to decipher its soul?
The exact meter they disburse means nothing to her;
it's not words you'll find here, not me dispensing
inspiration like aspirin, but water and its elemental kin —
all of us, the sea, the sun, the wind, and the rain,
joined to let-it-be as it is and has been; the moon
and earth, no words plash for a poet to own.

I want her to give back words, and, yes,
she can sit (not solicit) and listen.

We'll serenade her and play our tunes
like ripples in a lagoon, wind-felt signatures,
indecipherable at noon when everything is what is.

I See the Last of My Generation on an Auto Train

Like figures from Dante, they hobble, shoulders stooped
like questions marks propped in line, their walkers
and wives beside them. One man shaking a USA Today
mutters to his wife, *That's what's wrong with America.*
The TSA can't monitor its own employees!
His wife complains about Syria, *We should never*
get involved. Our stocks have never recovered.

I hold my mother's arm. Her balance is no good.
A young porter, blond with a sweet smile, asks,
May I help yoou all? I want to warn him
of the others, herds of them, following us,
some in wheelchairs, some with walkers,
parsing each step as if there's some abyss
they must miss. But he knows them well,
snowbirds who he coddles and pets for tips.
They pay him mightily for his biceps and smile.

In the dining car, we meet Ed and Edna.
They're headed to their gated community
where they're learning to play golf and can ride
in a golf cart anywhere — to shop, to dine, to play
golf or tennis — and everyone is retired, people
from all over the country, East, Midwest, South,
they come to be with others like them, a whole
generation to live a life of leisure and, one
by one, give up golf for croquet, clad in white
with their wooden hammers, to knock the ball
through the wickets for what's at stake.

My mother will return to her community too.
Ninety-six, she'll play bridge every Wednesday,
morning and afternoon, dine at the club.
swim at 8, aquatics for 20 minutes, attend
cocktail parties. A bluejay will steal
sunflower seeds she's put out for cardinals.
A catbird will shutter rain off its back.
No one will say they're dying. It's not polite.

We'll go to dinner. I'll ask her friends how
they are and hear about cataracts and dyspepsia,
legs aching and the waste of insomnia,
3 a.m. and nothing to read. Stars blink
in the skylight. No one to talk to, nothing
to do but wait for another morning in a long
line of mornings. Then dawn and coffee.

I'm here, one of them, retired,
pulling out my golf clubs,
slugging shots at the flags. Practice,
practice and what for? I know I should
not say a word. That's how I've been
raised. Be the good son. Be a nice man.
But is *this* what's left of us? The ones
marching down Route 80 to Montgomery,
sticking daisies in rifles barrels at the Pentagon,
listening to Hendrix while naked and enraptured in mud,
and being beaten bloody in the streets of Chicago?

The foursome, white-haired, in carts,
are testing with the latest Titleist driver.
Look, look how far it goes! I must wait—
my tee-off time in twenty minutes.
I putt a few balls on the practice green.
It's now I want to howl. I can't help it.
Oh, Ginsberg, what went wrong?
What went so horribly wrong?

One More Question for You, Dad

I thought, when I tossed your ashes
off the tenth tee, I was finished with you.
The wind didn't want them. Nor did it want me.

I'm here at 67, the age you sat on a balcony in Hawaii,
having played in a pro-am with a pro who never amounted to much,
and realized, as you looked at light fragmented in fronds
in the glimmering sunset, that the sun was setting for you.
You climbed the corporate ladder, becoming
Vice President of Zenith Radio Corporation,
someone who, when he arrived at work, doormen
greeted, "Morning, Mr. Spang" because
you were somebody. For seven years in a row, you were in
Who's Who In America and because of you
I was in there too. Men opened the door and
pressed the button of a private elevator that took
you to your suite of offices. You'd made it big.
Yet that night in the balmy air of the Pacific,
it seemed a rat race and the bait, d-Con.
After your second martini, you composed your resignation.

Retired, you built a house with a pool at the Yacht and Country Club,
right on the St Luce River, 10 minutes from the ocean,
and, there, in Florida with other men who had made it,
each morning drove in your golf cart to play 18 holes,
and in the evenings, made it to rounds of cocktail parties,
living off your retirement like you deserved it.

Here I am about to retire. I remember you hunched
over diamonds you faceted as a hobby,
appraising a stone for months before making a final cut
because you had all the time in the world to make the perfect break.
You dabbled in oil paintings too. They hang in the dining room,
splashes of red geraniums on the Roman steps, beautiful
next to Willi Bauer's twilight streets of Paris.

Then the unbidden came, four years of TIAs,
mini-strokes that left you off balance
so that as we walked into the dining room

at the club, you gripped my arm and smiled at all your friends
who, year by year, preceded or followed you to the grave until there
were no more of them and no more of you.

Here I am about to step into retirement, where work,
as I know it — the alarm at 5, the getting up, the shower,
the getting ready, being prepared — ends. I'm with others
who have left work behind, who talk about what was
as if they were living backwards. They don't speak
of how much their friends were worth — "nine million,"
as you used to do. They speak of hours alone.

Well, Dad, I'm not wanting the end of life
to be about riding off into the sunset at a resort,
about waiting for the next disequilibrium.
Can you help me out, Dad?

Come on, what do you do when you're no longer "Mr. Spang,"
when no one opens the door to let you in,
when no one even cares you once had a hole in one,
when diamonds lose their shimmer,
when the paint is dried on the palette,
when you are no one, when you can no longer
swing the club and cocktails spill from your hand?

I know what you did. You relied on it for years
like the taste of a lobster tail drowned in butter.
You savored the waiter who remembered you,
who knew you liked a martini, dry,
who acted as if, yes, you were still important.

That's not what I want. There must be something
else like a diamond inside of coal.
I'm waiting, Dad, for an answer.

I've got all the time in the world.

The Chain

Thirteen hours a day, six day jaunts,
Sergeant Henderson signs 'em up —
young men and woman who want
to serve, think they have the stuff.

He must meet quotas, ten at a whack.
Backyard shed, chain lock in place.
Henderson dismisses the flashback —
M-16 bore fist-sized holes through her body.

He signs 'em up, one at a time
at the strip mall by Wal-Mart;
strapping, confident, sincere,
he wins them over. It's an art —

his job. They have nothing to fear.
Backyard shed, chained, lock in place.
Seven hundred bullets per minute
riddled every bone in her face.

A boy, 18, asks him, *Numbers of body bags?*
His M-16, fully-automatic, wasn't saying.
Nor was he. Three quotas missed — lost his touch.
In the shed, he hung himself, chain and dog tag.

Nate Writes His Own Short Story

I want Nate, a tall lanky sophomore
who hates to read — and, well, writing
is not his thing — to compose one scene
in a story — to use his imagination.
I ask, "Where is your character?"
He smiles. "Hawaii," clearly pleased with his setting.
"Good," I say and ask, "Does he live on the beach?"
Nate nods.
"What's he doing?"
"Waking up . . . . It's morning, early morning."

I'm getting somewhere!

"Have him go to the window — what does he see?"
He puts his finger to his lips.
"A woman in a white dress."
"Perfect! What is she doing?"
"She's walking her dog."
"What type?"
"A Jack Russell terrier," he says, grinning.
"Good, that's great! Write it down!"

Nate does not want to write about the beach,
to place one word after another on a blank page.
He wants to *be* on the beach, to walk toward
the woman in the white dress who will see him,
virile and handsome, smiling at her. She will unleash
her terrier. It will prance across the sand to him.
He will bend and ruffle its wiry mane.
He will follow it back to the woman who offers
her hand, and they will walk away in
a story where no one writes about what happens next
because no one is worried about what will happen next.

The sun is rising on the Pacific. The palms
shiver in the balmy breeze. The two of them,
silent and sure, head off down the beach like bathers
in a Georges Seurat painting. It's natural
that one scene or the next will wash away
like little dots of sand. No one will ever read it.
Nate and the girl are far down the beach —
specks — when the bell rings. Nate stands;
nothings on the page. He's outta here,
gone to American History. Already the next
class like a tide sweeps into the room.

The Nixon Years, a Multiple Choice

The student pokes his pencil over the word "Hunt" —
this word scrabble worth one-eighth his grade.
He's not sure. It's just a name.
It doesn't matter if it's Ellsberg
or Hunt, presiding over
the Watergate hearings. What matters
is getting it right on the test
so he can fling a ball in the net,
make a name for himself.

After all the hours in front of the TV
watching men in perfectly
pressed shirts astutely deliver lies
until one man in dark-framed glasses
paused and says "hush funds"
it doesn't seem right
to reduce history to points.

The question in June 1973 was not
a multiple choice worth five points.
National Guard troops shot students —
who *died* for what they believed.

Now names like Eldridge Cleaver
are worth as much as Spiro Agnew.
Those assassinated in 1968
can be either "Humphrey and Wallace"
or "Kennedy and King."   Five points each.
Five points for Ethel pleading, *Give him air, give him air.*
Five points for Detroit consumed in flames.

Does it matter if Earl Warren or Henry Kissinger
was Chief Justice of the Supreme Court?
Or that 4,000 or 58,000 soldiers died in Vietnam?
Names. Numbers. 40 points.

The sagging jowls of Sam Ervin shuddered
as he pointed the tip of a pencil at John Dean,
probing the shape of truth
as Dean testified that a president assured
him the office of the president can do no wrong,

that a president can dismiss anyone as easily as
the student can erase "Kennedy"
and replace it with "Wallace"
and make the grade, start the game—
another game of numbers.

"Facing It" as AP Multiple Choice Questions

Yusef, when the AP exam asks
about the "black face" fading into stone as
(A) *an attempt to resist emotion*, I want to scream.

When you say, "I turned this way—
the stone lets me go" the AP students are not
asked of the dead comrades
with their intestines in their hands and one
arm blown off—bleeding out—
but are asked if it is an example of
    (A) allegory or
    (B) personification.

Would you tell them how stone
pleads with you to let the horror go,
to be done with Mr. Death? Would you
tell them it is not allegory, but gore?

But the exam wants them to analyze "The mirror like
quality of the granite wall" and how it
allowed the speaker to experience
all of the following—are you ready, Yusef? —
EXCEPT
    (a) self-effacement
    (b) self-awareness
    (c) self-respect
    (d) the illusion of having been transformed
    (e) identification with the memorized veterans

You know the answer, Yusef? Come on, tell them,
draw it in the mud with your jammed rifle butt.

Supercilious

A common goldfish, Gus,
with tail fins like silk banners,
confined in his tank,
swishes back and forth.
I discuss *The Great Gatsby*,
the book, with students, avid for an A
but vaguely distracted
by Gus, his inward turning,
back and forth
as they pore through text,
learning about characters who lived in some
bubble of time they'd as soon forget,
learning about language —
hard mouth and supercilious manner —
with long words I insist they know,
words whose fate is as doomed
as Gatsby's. Words befuddle them.
Several fail the test. One day
when I'm out ill, while words
slip away, they turn their Fs
on Gus and dump white board cleaner
into his tank. Despite Kenny,
a punctilious boy, hovering over
the tank, guarding it,
pleading *Stop, stop,*
everyone laughs at Gus
writhing this way and that
because, as one girl explains,
our idea was to get a laugh —
or more of a prank, actually.
We all just thought, hm, whatever,
25 cent fish at Petco.

Miracle

"See it?" a priest asks, pointing
to a likeness in chiaroscuro
I can barely make out:
baby Jesus swaddled in his mother's arms
in a third-story window.
It takes me time to decipher it.

In psych class, I never quite
made out those twin images embedded in one —
the witch and the beautiful lady.
The seen and unseen baffled my eye.

On this street corner, shoppers shove by,
their arms laden with sacks
stuffed from sales — ten dollars
for a hand-woven shirt worth fifty,
linens at bargain basement prices —
you can get what you want,
stores practically giving away goods.

But what *do* I want?

A friend asks what I'm gawking at.
The priest motions to the window.

She screws her head sideways, says,
"It looks like pigs kissing,"
tracing their snouts with her index finger.

She wants to shop, to beat the rush,
to indulge in Macy's red and gold displays.

"Why doesn't some janitor," she asks, "Windex it?"

Is the image like stained glass in a cathedral,
the same inside as out —
Jesus' chubby arms grasping for Madonna?

My friend tugs at my sleeve.
"You wouldn't believe the sales on iPods!"

Nothing's in my arms, no gifts for family.

I'm trying to make up my mind

when the priest nudges me and says,
"I'm not much for miracles, but I do
like watching those who are."

He points to a woman rubbing her rosary
as if, with her ecstatic fingers, she'll
grind the beads to dust.

He smiles. "I'm shopping, too—
to purchase a little faith from the faithful."

Coffee by Design

A man leans on a table sipping coffee
dark roast, strong
the New York Times spread out —
old news: a bomb,
earthquake, more dread.
Dawn uncurls itself
to front the facts,
the essence of this hour.

Ten paces away, another sips his coffee
decaf, cream and two sugars.
The daily devotional before him —
Today, *serenity;* tomorrow, *release.*

The white effacement of the building
yields to dawn — its mouth wide open —
erubescent splashing the exterior.

This ritual continues for years —
coffee, news, devotion
while dawn undoes itself.

Portland

Two skateboarders bomb down Congress Street,
avoiding potholes that swallow SUVs—
past Longfellow, sturdy on his throne—
picking up speed, past
Reny's latest sales windows,
a teacher with a Coffee by Design,
threading in and out of the Pride Parade,
past the Time and Temperature Building
—its digital eyes blinking 1:00 and 70 degrees,
toward Nike, Goddess of Victory, who
unfurls her robe like a topsail, glides from
her pedestal, and sails along with them,
careening across the ribs of roads,
by First Parish, past City Hall,
its clipper ship tilted eastward,
its grand old clock torqued
by the ineffable tide—past the firehouse,
building momentum toward Munjoy Hill—
swept by the wind's will—
Nike's topsail vaulting them upward,
past the Cathedral of the Immaculate Conception,
past Etz Chaim Synagogue,
past Green Memorial AME Zion Church,
shadowing the underground railroad,
cresting the Eastern Prom, skittering past
a Sudanese boy dancing a soccer ball on his toe,
a girl in a purple hijab flipping cartwheels,
and a terrier tugging his owner
toward ferries stitching across Casco Bay,
and there, gazing at the blue sheen,
the skateboards sweep down
the hill toward the lashing, lulling sea
by an elderly couple who bid them well,
winged with Nike behind them—full sail
off the boat ramp, over lobster boats,

over Little Diamond, Long Island, and Chebeague
past Two Lights — a victory lap —
headed back toward England, Ireland,
Italy, France, back to Somalia,
to Africa, Palestine, back to Israel,
to Greece, Turkey, back to Cambodia,
to Thailand, Vietnam, Japan, back
to the crest of Congress where they will slide again
down the ribs of this city, this port called home.

The Length of Your Heart

— for Marita O'Neill

You read to me a selection from Charles Dickens'
A Tale of Two Cities, the part where
Sydney Carton, a destitute barrister,
implores gentle Lucie *to hear him.*
Pale and trembling, she listens
as he tells her she is *the last dream of his soul*
how she kindled in him, in *the heap of ashes*
that he was, a flame. As you finish the passage,
I look in your eyes, teary, filled
with compassion. You whisper to me,
"Isn't that lovely?" And it is.

But not as lovely as you are,
filled with the word, the terrible
and tender power of language.
Oh, I'm not Sydney Carton,
offering up a *last supplication*
in my misdirected life,
entreating you to hold *sacred*
the last avowal of my heart
because, let's face it: I'm gay.

But I will, as Sydney, hold onto
how much you love
language — as much what is said
as who actually said it — and trust
the truth, be it hard
as the invisible face of a prisoner
caged like an animal in Guantanamo
or tender as Anthony's supplication
to those who would just as soon
stab him as listen to his words,

and how your students — I count
myself as one — find the heart
to go on and carry with them
how you bend over their words
and ask them to find
in the prison of their hearts
a door into the sanctuary of life.

III.

A White Mask in Venice on the Piazza San Marco

After a photograph "Reflections 3, Venice, Italy" by Jeanette Phillipps

Like a mirage, she lingers among the loggia
with their arched porches like rows of Ns,
each with a door to what is and has been.

With her mango-yellow coat buttoned
as if like fog she'll melt into the lagoon,
a ghostly hint of another face:

of men kneeling before the Doge who stood
on the steps of his palace, neither smiling
nor frowning since his eyes were closed.

Lucia, his beautiful daughter offered
on a golden platter her blue eyes to a suitor
who could not accept "no", could not let her go.

Behind her lashes, a forlorn heart,
a forbidden lover, the face of a man
who wept at the sight of a hill of daffodils;

the man who turned, not once,
but twice, his back on Christ;
the face of Napoleon who kneeled to

a winged lion who purred to his touch.
Her face, a saint whose eyes she offered
like blue gems to anyone who wanted

to peer inside what might have been.
With a scarf coiled on her neck like
a red boa, she unbuttoned her coat

like a lens on a camera, fluttered her lids
this long last day of Carnival. Soon no one
will eat steak, pork, lamb or fowl.

She'll hover in the piazza, open her eyes,
click her heels. Revelers vanish. Alone,
she'll smile: *there's no place like gone*.

What to Tell?

The scrambled eggs had not scrambled.
The phone and my daughter called,
"Kirsten's house caught fire!"

Kirsten whose house she stayed at on overnights,
gabbing about boy bands and has-beens.

I drove the ten miles to her house.

Yellow police tape slung like bandages
from tree to tree to one lone stake.
Beams bent inward. A slab of a roof tilted
and between, a gap like a jaw smoldering.

There was a chill and lazy smoke.

After a bystander told me the story,
I wanted, on the drive back, to make up
something about a family caught off-guard,
staving off flames, desperate, one
after another failing, overcome, the heat
consuming them. I wanted to tell
of a mother who had hand-sewn costumes
for Halloween that year,
who my daughter told me
wished was *her* mom—
who perished—

not to tell of a mother
who had purchased a gallon of gasoline,
yet owned no lawnmower,
and a revolver, yet lived in a gated community;
who stepped into her bedroom in the blink
of a January night, closed the door and shot her husband
point-blank in the head, then tiptoed to her daughter's

bedroom and did the same; who lastly, doused
the house with gasoline—furniture, hallways, beds,
stairs, carpet—and sat in an easy chair,
downstairs, struck a match and tossed it,
and then shot herself.

We never speak of it—
as we drive by: our silence as silent as
the match before it struck the floor.

Two Teens, a Town and Kudzu

Based on a photograph "Knoxville, Summer, 2001" by David Hilliard

Hip-high in it, the white waistband
of his jockey shorts slung low on his hips,
and below them, the fresh blue of new jeans
and like a flower poking
out of green, his shirtless body with nipples
like stamen that you could kiss
if you were a bee but, you're a camera,
focused on the whole of him —
hair the color of rust — fingers holding
a large Krystal soda, and the morning light
dappling through the weeds grown
so high around him there is no stopping it.

This is how lust flings itself
on a loved one who lies there,
shirtless, and those splayed vines
grab the giant root of a pine
and extend their fingers, caress
it all the way up over the whole
until it's kudzu, vine and leaves
aroused with no compunction:
wanting everything regardless
of consent.

It merely wants light and
more light, a sweet pea canopy
of loving too much, smothering
love until it lives less,
a carcass of trunk and branch and stem.

Up the hillside, another teen holds
his super-size soda and glances
back wistfully. His brown
hair delicate on his cheeks, white
T-shirt like a petal merged in green.

Beyond them, down the valley,
the kudzu snakes toward town,
a few petals of houses and a steeple,
forms that could be overrun
in a summer, maybe two.
They stand apart, distinct,
the way the one teen is unaware
that the other moans and wants
to reach back, yes, and embrace him.

The shutter yields — there they all are,
caught in the might be of the moment,
bodies in kudzu or the edge of kudzu
creeping where it must.

Goodbye

The flicker of light
in an upper window — TV news,
 all day long, talk, talk, talk.
A woman stares at her wrist —
a watch with no hands.
A man clings to the streetlight —
his ship is sinking fast.
A policeman peers at the opposite corner.
No one there. Only red going on forever.
The rain pelts the window.
The sky is ripped open. It can't last.
A radio plays 'Jailhouse Rock.'
It's November 22, 1963.
An umbrella hangs by the door.
The officer pulls up his collar.
Two hours more.
The ship shudders.
There's a flop. Man overboard.
A light goes out in the window.
This storm may never pass.

On Time

Do you hear the soft *ohhs* in the mist—
these sighs of God?

They miss the man—late,
no doubt, who taps at his Rolex:

years tumble forward—already 2020,
2060; tomorrow flattens this day.

A solitary pigeon pecks at a crumb,
lifts, undulant in gray.

What condenses from this mist? —
intonations of *too late, too late;*

or hands on his watch like I Ching,
little sticks of metaphor ?

Another Night at the A-1 Diner

It's cheap. Piss-warm coffee.
Three forks hang from the dropped ceiling.

March batters at the windows.
Let me in. Let me in.

At 8:47 I found a key on the table.
No note. My son, 17, had left for good.

His room heaped with DVDs, socks —
and a photograph of a robin, gift of his foster dad —
come spring when the robin comes, I'll visit —
a promise he gave. Then he died.

I packed it up, put it away, made room for — *what?*

Grief slides into the booth, spreads his thick hands
on the table and taps his fingers.

Not now. Get outta here.

He shrugs, *I own this place.*

There's a chrome counter, lemon pie in the rack and red vinyl
swivel stools that my son used to spin on like a rotor.

I sip coffee. Grief stares into my eyes.
He plucks down a buck for a refill, says nothing.

The Purpose of Plagiarism

Does anyone care about the lines in my 1965 edition
of *The Norton Anthology of Modern Poetry?*

With one thousand seven hundred forty-two
pages of poems and nearly forty lines per page,
who would know, who would care
if I took a few as my own?

These little lines are crowded together
like tenants in a boarding house,
shoved into rooms, one on top of another.
They don't even know each other.
Dead men stuck next to the living.
None written by me.

I never said,
I have known the inexorable sadness of pencils or
Our single purpose was to walk through snow or
I know a little language of my cat or
I have just come down from my father
but I might, given time, have coaxed
them into verse and claim them as my own.

Back in 1972 James Dickey strutted on stage
with tattooed cowboy boots colored
like the biceps of a Hell's Angel and told
students at Vanderbilt the highest compliment
he'd been paid was by a student who so loved his words
that he stole his book. He rejoiced
that some kid lifted his words off a shelf.

One could do worse than steal a line.
One could start a whole career grabbing
lines from *the first cave, the first farm,
the first sage* – there I have done it again.
It's like a close-out sale.

I'm in good company. *Overhead, the match*
burns out. The machine gun bullets hit
my wife in the legs. It may be painful
absconding with verse, but these are just words.

What good are they crowded in an anthology?
Quick, somebody do something with them.

Neighborhoods

are like memories you'd rather forget.
They lead to Willow and Elm, to streets
memorized, streets that turn
the unimaginable into dead ends
that do not end, streets
that spill into footpaths that drop
into ravines and woods —
like bad dreams — past a boulder
where revenge has set up ranch
and is waiting, his pistol poised.

A figure darts out of a hedge.
He's quick like a dagger.

"Hey, officer! Bang, you're dead."
He's playing cops and robbers.

You know when his mother
arrives home from work.

You breathe, just breathe.

Most people drive main streets,
never turn into the unknown
where — who knows? — it's a dead end.

They want to get to the home they know,
no matter the gridlock, no matter the wait.

Useless

I'm tired of words that taste of d-Con.
Maybe it isn't the taste.
Perhaps, it's how they look
like the ribs of snow
worn thin by winter?
Maybe it's me — it's age,
the taste of sweet and sour,
mostly sour, in my mouth.

Words used to be like lovers,
winsome and handsome,
that slip under sheets,
nibble and nuzzle,
hands all over, wanting me
as much as I wanted them.

I wish words were like they were in 1963:
It's Friday night at Dwayne Street School,
There's a dance and Judy Selman puts 45s
one at a time. We *twist the night away*!

Where do old words go? Face it:
They're as useless as 45s, as black and white
TV, as the Twist— old and done for.

Whole nations are under the age of 29.
They chant, *Freedom, freedom,*
stand on tanks, tell the old rulers
to scram, and even plunge into bullets,
willing to die for words.

My body is not their body. My body
remembers Birmingham —
the hoses, the dogs, the children,
the thousands of children that Bull Conner's
white tank and batons could not keep back.
Freedom. Freedom.

I want to believe again.

Let's face it, words want to be young.
They want us to believe in them,
love them, nibble on them—
even if they taste of death.

Getting It Right

As one accepting a new faith,
I converted to masturbation,
morning, afternoon, and evening.
Only on breaks, after basketball practice,
after finding the x in an equation,
did I recite

I believe in God, The father almighty,
Creator of heaven and earth . . .
And, ahh, *Jesus Christ, God's only Son,*
Our Lord . . .who . . . .

Ten days to memorize the Apostles' Creed,
and be an adult member of the church,
yet all I could think of was sex.
I'd prop my hands on my desk.
Temptation called me like a first alert
in my pants, poking up at all hours. I'd say,

Conceived by the unholy spirit,
Suffered under Pontius Pilate,

Five days left, in health class, Miss Sterling
pointed at a two- foot-long penis on a chart.
She jabbed it and asked as if she'd
seen mine rising like a hand,
"Where, Mr. Spang, is the vans deferens?"
This, her autopsy for sex. My penis was

Crucified, dead and buried.

Three days to memorize five lines.
All that came to mind was Pat Boone
in his white bucks singing
On a day like today, I pass the time away . . .
singing my heart out in the shower,

under the pressure of warm water
for the seventh straight day
in a row my erection
Rose and ascended into heaven,
as I knew it.

The day I trudged to the minister's study
prepared to fail, never to be a member
of the holy Apostolic Church,
never to have my sins, accumulating mightily,
forgiven, never to realize the resurrection of the body.

A black sleeve ushered me to a chair.
It looked suspiciously like an electric chair.
Under a picture of crucifixion, the priest asked,
"You're a member of the undefeated team,
the center, if I'm correct?"

"Yes," I offered, awaiting the inquisition.

He folded his hands between his legs.

"You want to shoot some hoops?" he asked.

"Sure," I said. He doffed his robe and I noticed
his broad shoulders and his white sneakers.

We played 21, hot, sweaty,
faking right, left, grabbing rebounds,
shoving, jigger stepping, leaping high
for a shot at the rim, until he wiped his brow
and smiled, "That's it," patting me on the back.

We sat on a stoop, his tall slender body
next to mine, drinking lemonade,
talking about the game, the moves,
the pleasure of a ball swishing,
his playing guard — first string — in college.

He took a deep breath and laughed,
"It's great getting out on the court again,
seeing I still have the moves."

I told him that he was good, really good.
He laughed and picked up the ball
and twirled it on one finger.

I understood *the resurrection of the body,*
the life everlasting, seated here
at the right hand of the Father

talking about Wilt Chamberlain, all 7 feet of him,
scoring 100 in one game, amazed at what he could do,
talking like men who belonged,
who played the same game,
who spoke the same language.

The Doors

Sprawled in the Rite-Aid parking lot,
an elderly man in red paisley shirt and pleated slacks
lies there as if reclining on the beach.

I nearly run over him,
then park and hurry over.

"Do you want help?"

He cranes his head sideways.

"Yes. Thank you. That would be nice."

Outside the glass doors, four Rite-Aid staff, worried, watch us.

The man's body, long and angular, bony,
concave, rises uneasily, his weight drawn
backward as if he's on a ship listing horribly.

I lean him forward. His body lurches back.
It knows *this was it.*

I'm going down with him, I think. *Damn.*
I glance at the four employees.
A burgundy cane like a question mark
sits two feet away.

A young boy, sprinting across the lot,
picks up the cane and grabs like angels
do in movies the other arm of the man.

The man, his gaunt face inches from mine,
the paper-thin skin on his cheekbones
and the faraway gaze in his eyes,
makes me think how he must yearn
to be in silken water, buoyant,
swimming past all this.

I thought of my father,
neuropathy numbing his legs,
holding onto to me as we took
the stairs down to the club dining room,
his friends watching, holding their breath
as each leg cast off each step and hovered
in mid-air before finding, yes, the stair.

I feel my own knees, worn from running, beneath me.

I asked if he wants to go into the store.
He says, "Yes, that would be good. But over *there*,"
pointing to the paved ramp.

We — the boy and I — usher him there.

He mutters, "I shouldn't have tried it,"
glaring at the curb.

He stepped on the ramp: it too tips him.
We catch him and right him.

An employee asks, "Shall we call an ambulance?"

He shuffles along, ignoring her.
One foot, then another. Baby steps, scuffing
along with us holding him, as he tilts
to one side, then another, and finally rights himself.

Steady, half-way up the ramp, he says,
"Thank you — that's fine," dismissing us
with a wave of one hand, puts his cane
firmly down, leans on it, and stands there,
not moving, taking a breath, focused —
staring at the sliding glass doors.

"Are you all right?" I ask.

"Yes," he replies. The boy lets go of one arm.
I tentatively let go of the other
as I did — long ago — of the arm of my son on his bike.

The man's body presses forward,
eyes riveted on the store, past the four employees
through the doors that, as if at his command,
magically slide open to let him pass.

Enough

Turn the lamp on, turn it off,
it wobbles — tilting like it's
history, not unlike

my mother, nine decades now.
She plays golf, 18 holes,
swims lengths of a pool — an hour —,
takes her nightly walk — a mile up and back.
Each day, her feet shuffle —
her leathery legs wrinkled, bony,
muscles worn, her body but a wisp
as if gravity forgot like petals of a poppy
she's there and may, at any moment,
let her flutter away.

Is that how it is — the arthritis,
hands clawed, feet splayed,
the gradual withering, the lightness,
and then, the letting go?

The lamp toppled over, cracked.
Had it enough? I super-glued it.
On my nightstand, it lights
as it always has. It does not,
as I think it should, admit,
Enough is enough.

O mother, how is it you putter
at the counter, fix Waldorf salads –
slice the apples, add the tiny marshmallows,
walnuts and raisins; mash your twice-
baked potatoes; sauté chicken
in béarnaise sauce; set the table;
light the two candles in their bell jars;
and wait for guests full of talk
and promise of tomorrow?

IV.

Not Just Pornography

Is it my age that makes me appreciate how bodies work?
My knee gives out halfway up the hill.
I cannot twist off the aspirin cap.
My feet look like strangers in another land.

I admire how the boy outside
the supermarket hops in his car,
turns the key and is off.

Any wonder when I look at pornography,
it's like viewing another species
enjoying what flesh has to offer us
as if pleasure were there for the taking,
as if lust ignites the veins and makes
us twenty-one with no one to stop us.

Oh, I know porn has a bad reputation,
these endless loops of fevered men
on fevered men, unbuttoning shirts and pants
and tossing them aside like Adam
with no Eve. The lovers make love
as if love has to be made, the touch,
the kiss, the reaching, the zipper
and then, oh yes, the rhapsody.

This is not something simply for harlots.
It's how we came to be made:
this act of loving, of letting oneself go.

I watch them and imagine how it was
when my body was always ready
to make love by a river,
in a tent, under a willow.

I wonder if the guy in the film
is displaying what he learned pays
the rent. Or is it his wanting someone
to notice, yes, he has what it takes.

He performs like an Olympic gymnast—
up, down, flips, turns. He may smile.
He may look far off at a wall,
as if his mother knows what he's doing
and wants her cut, or his father sees
what has become of his boy
and wants nothing to do with him.

I don't want to be reminded how abused,
how lost he could be. A porn star
in a campground on Long Island recounted
how he came to the campground with his sleeping
bag and food to beat his addiction.
He told of his salad days, his black Maserati,
the condo in Hollywood, movie after movie.
He had to keep it up for so long, he reverted
to uppers and, when he came down, he wanted
up. So it went, up and down, in and out,
year by year, his career on the line to stardom
until lines crept around his eyes and he could
no longer rise to every occasion.

I saw him in an early film. His dark thick hair,
his toned body, his manhood, large, ample.
For the whole hour, he never smiled.
He worked hard. Love, a job,
he did it well. I felt sorry for him,
clicked off the film, preferring
him drawn and haggard, suffering,
struggling to return to a body
where love is more than anatomy.

Instead, I watched two young kids,
barely used to their adult bodies,
who did not know better,
amateurs showing off what came naturally.
They laughed and cuddled and kissed.
They joked and hammed for the camera.
It was sweet. I wanted to tell them,
"Yes, you have it right. Don't make love

a drama. Enjoy it." They only needed
to hold each other, as they did,
and ride passion as far as it lasted.

As a keepsake, they'd have the film
to look at when they are old, settled,
and embarrassed they'd made it.
By then the mortgage will be overdue.
No one will remember them.
"There we are," they will say.
"Look how easy it was."

It will not be pornography.
It will be how love graces the body,
how, ageless, lust sings in our veins,
rises like an everlasting hurrah
as young as those boys whose bodies,
sweet and poignant, cry out *yes, yes.*

The Boy at the Screen Door

Based on photograph "Norm's birthday, 2001" by David Hilliard

Head against the screen door,
soda in one hand, insouciant, staring in.
Her breast covered with her hands,
modest, not looking toward him but wary.
He's waiting for her to speak.

She's sitting on a bed in a cottage
by a lake. It's summer. It's hot.
It's his birthday. He's seventeen.

On a wall, a stuffed squirrel poised
to scurry off. No mark
of the bullet that broke its back.

Across, a mirror where
the raw body of the young man,
a boy, seething with yearning, waits.

Anything could happen.

This is a photograph.
Someone is standing in the room.
His lens is pointed at the girl
and the boy. What we see
is what he wants us to see: the boy,
his eyes fixed on the girl,
her milky breasts against her tanned hands.
The sanguine lake beyond the porch —
framed by someone we never see.

What, I ask you, do you want to happen?

For her to hurry and dress so they can
meet their friends waiting for them?

For him to open the door and to tell
her how beautiful she is?
For them to stay as they are,
waiting for the other to move?

What of the unseen in the room?

Does the photographer open the door,
take the young man's hand, as the girl
dresses and silently walks away?

Perhaps he slides next to her?
Perhaps, the porch is empty,
the rooms vacant?

I want the young man to speak.
May I come in?
She says, *yes.*
For them to look at their bodies —
his broad shoulders and two nipples,
small and erect, on his hairless chest,
her long neck and two nipples,
wide and thick, on her milky breasts.
Nipples pressed against nipples. Ahh.

The door slaps shut. One fly preens
on the screen. The squirrel slips down
the wall toward an acorn under
the bed. The camera's eye closes.

All there is
            is breathing.

Affirmations

I walk around the yard.
I count daffodils, the older ones
with eight flowers clumped together, their noses
stuck in different directions as if, by each of them
facing another direction, they capture all the sun
can give them. Lupine have sprung up too,
thick and sturdy, along with wormwood,
which has sent its sprigs, invaded nearly two feet of garden,
surrounding a solitary tulip. The delphiniums are upright and
lamb's ear has shoots sticking up from the flattened
silver brown debris. The hosta noses up,
its green poker tightly woven and stern,
same as the first sprouts of oriental lilies,
something satyrs would admire.
The hillside is splashed with yellow, orange, white
daffodils — such optimism, such hope
as if they were messengers who see in themselves
another life like yellow narcissus
by the brook, leaning over: it's love at first sight.

What We Have Unsaid

> — *Hey, wanted to wish you a happy New Year, bro —*
> *you catch the Bears game?*
> — *No.*
> — *Lost. Season's over — for them.*
> — *Too bad. Oh, by the way, your business okay?*
> — *Don't ask.*

Our room, beds split by a nightlight,
yours by the door, mine by the wall,
seventeen years coming, going,

dress for school, for church, for guests,
undress in the breath of night,
our dreams rippling the surface,

eight-year-old faces like grapefruits — mumps;
perpetual erections — whispered regrets,
our particular lusts,

your spleen ruptured by that fall —
broken branch;
later my thumb torn in half

from the lid of a peach can. Our bodies
betrayed us, the blossoms of ache,
the ones we loved not loving us.

Yet, in the last seconds
of a big game your one-handed grab
of my pass — touchdown!

We won it all — that moment,
an atonement for all the not-quites —
and what father called *the real world*:

you, a salesman, convincing customers
of wants they never knew they had;
I, a minister, unconvinced, doubtful

even of the existence of fingers
that could grab that ball
as yours did, stretched out

knowing we had no time left—
you, now, on antidepressants.
And I? *"Don't ask."*

The Moon on a Quiet Night

I used to write by your light.

When was it?

Thirty years ago in a room where
I never pulled the shade
and stood naked at the window
looking out on the South Branch.
The silver thread of river unraveled
in the valley that stretched miles
into the blue-grey urging of the hills.

The moonlight was hushed then,
too shy to speak.

The rich groaned in cities far from me.
The stock market plummeted 45%,
their grand schemes imploded.
There was another war.
fifty-eight thousand dead.

Tonight, miles away, downtown,
the protest against Wall Street is
in its second week — ten tents in Lincoln Park;
people huddled by a fire, warming their hands;
"Tax the Rich" wrapped like a bandage on an iron fence.

This time of night few cars drive by.

Who cares?

Light on the sleek bank
of our back yard seems flimsy
on the fallen snow like it's lost all hope.

Is it too late?

No one is listening.

Can we talk?

I made love once under your light.
I swam naked through your light.
I nearly drown in your light.

I paid no heed to money.

I had nothing then. A small job, a room,
a yearning to be larger than I was,
to stand by the river,
to proclaim august sounds
in the chill of night,
to know someone was listening,
if it were only your face glistening
in the water, old shape-shifter
I could count on to be changeless
in the ever-changing night.

The rich may get richer.
They may even claim the moon
is not the moon, but a placard
peppered with bullet holes.

So what can we count on?

The rising or the falling?
The expanding and contracting?
The ups and downs?

Are you listening?

I'm writing to your light that, the other night,
spilled on the slender fissure in the creek,
a glint on its watery surface like a yes.

Waking the Crow

for Michael Macklin

What did you say as you walked away?
Oh, nothing.

That night slips on its noose when you sleep?
I'd say it plainer.

That the sun rises on Islesboro, tapping thick fingers
      on the cabin you built by hand,
        to write your last book of poems,
        to see if you're there?
What are you talking about?

Death.
Mine?

Yes, it arrived on the night you danced wildly with two teens,
      boys — poets like you — near the fire,
      your burly frame light on your feet,
      whooping, singing, playing your guitar.
      The next morning . . .
Where was I? I bet they wanted to know.

Two boys searching — your door unlocked — found you, silent,
immovable.
Shit. That must'a tore em up.

It did.
Hey, how are you holding up?

I'm lost because I loved how, at any moment, you charmed
      anyone with your mellifluous voice. Your tongue, magic.
I was pretty good, wasn't I?

Damn good.
What's up now?

Not you. Envelopes, a leather journal, a scrap of paper with your
        scrawls, notes for a book, poems, on a nightstand.
I don't like this.

Nor I, nor the 38 who at Local Sprouts sipped coffee, downed a brew
        or two, remembering you, wanting you there, telling
        your stories of Italy, Ireland and the kids, always the kids.
It's over?

Yep.
Damn.

Can I ask you something?
Shoot. I have lots of time.

Does the morning, when you'd be on the porch sipping coffee,
        communing with crows, inhaling your first cigarette, last forever?
You think?

I do. I bet your last full day on the mountain, May, the long stone wall
        in the morning and the field beyond, the sky full of itself . . . .
        and you . . . .
Me? What about me?

You taking it all in — the coffee, the nicotine, the coming on of green,
        taking it in. Is that what you did?
Come to think of it, yeah, I did. And hey, that crow, in the birch — where'd he go?

Still up there, I imagine.
Hmm. Funny how it works out.

What?
You end up where you belong.

Hiber Nation

is an isolated country
down an unmarked road
where traffic never moves.
All GO signs say STOP.
The one highway in does not lead out.
Zzzz the nation's capital.
Rip Van Winkle its hero.
When Ambition was overthrown,
It-Can-Wait became the sole political party.
Extroverts are extinct.
There's no need to hurry.
Expect everyone to be
where they were yesterday.
The news is no news.
The national sport is snoring.
Clocks are banned.
Nodding off is a norm.
Getting ahead is left behind.
Don't ask for directions.
All roads lead nowhere.
Its one restaurant is closed,
the coffee left on the counter,
its steam forming a lazy S
that seems to say *Shush*.
There's no government,
only an interim dream
of might and maybe.
It's not on any map
but can be found
if one doesn't want
to go anywhere.
It's worth the trip —
an introvert's delight.

Slender Light

We learn to love by what we lose to gain.
The door left open, the dark empty room.
We find our way by leaving what remains.

Dare to hold the wind. It cannot be retained.
The shutter closes the heart of the moon.
We learn to love by what we lose to gain.

In whose wallet dare we find what sustains?
The golden tooth glints in the heiress's tomb.
We find our way by leaving what remains.

A Casanova in the penthouse complains
he's out of touch; the skies too blue.
We learn to love by what we lose to gain.

Climb Everest, touch heaven and name
a peak for some dying niece or nephew.
We find our way by leaving what remains.

Grasp the slender lightness of fame —
how little we know of what we do.
We learn to love by what we lose to gain
and learn the way by leaving what remains.

Simply Wonderful

For Dr. Richard Steinmann, (1925 - 2006)
   a founder of Maine Gay and Lesbian Political Alliance
   (now Equality Maine)

Twice my age, you invited me to lunch, bought me a hotdog,
stared at me and shook your head.

"Lovely, lovely," you said, so I looked around to see what you saw.

I realized you saw *me*.

I expected to discuss aging — you were renowned in the field.
You veered to homosexuality, to a land I'd imagined dimly.

"Oh, my god," you said.
You undressed me with your eyes.
"Are you sure you're not gay?"

 I averted my eyes.
"Pretty sure."

"Too bad, my dear boy."

You inquired about Watergate and civil rights.
Whatever I said you nodded, "Yes, yes, my dear boy, exactly right,"
even though I had no idea what I was saying.
What mattered, as you held me in your gaze, was that my life was unfolding.

As you drove me, June 1977, to Deering Park, past midnight,
pointed at the dim figures standing under ancient oaks,
and said, "Maybe your life will change. Here's the only place
some sad souls can find a moment's pleasure."
Then, you took me to a gay bar, hidden like a jewel on a side street.
Under red and blue disco lights, I danced until sweat poured off like diamonds.

We talked about the attraction of one man to another,
of the shame I felt, of what I dared not admit,
of your marriage before you knew, and mine, as it was,
and of our children. We met often in a sports bar off Exchange.
By October 1994, you retired, and I untold my lie.

In our hours together, you told me many stories,
that came back to one story as if it were yesterday:
I'm swimming laps in the university pool . . . .
This gorgeous, —you sigh— lad is standing right there
above me as I hung on the ladder staring up at him, his beautiful body
right there and this lovely — how do you say it?? —cock!
I nearly drown from desire, the simple pleasure of seeing him,
and, amazingly, he wanted me. He took me by the hand to the dressing room.
It was wonderful, simply wonderful!

Richard, you told the story of love as if you knew no man
— not straight, not handsome, not gay, not young—
had a key to it. Love was a door any of us could pass though.
Some knew from the start. Some took longer.
You waited for us to find the right love,
so we could swim the length of the pool,
step up the ladder where you, older, smiling, standing in your Speedo,
can take us by the hand—your foot wedged in the door,
assuring it stays open to the place we call *Pride*.

The Tail

Some people cut them, snip them, find them
intrusive like a handbag knocking off
a Royal Doulton on the coffee table.

But when she climbs into bed with me,
nuzzling against my flank and tells me
in her Morse Code, her dits and dahs,

Good morning, I know the truth in tails.
Her eyes, as mine, can deceive.
Yet her tail taps out *I'm here* just as

Marconi wireless operators tapped out *SOS*
on the sinking Titanic. A loved one
can hide *I'm pissed.*

You neglected me. with beguiling smiles.
Whole agonies — *I want to die. I want
you dead* — can lie like an iceberg under eyelids.

How much easier it would be if we had a tail.
Do you love me? *Thump?*
Well, all right, do you want to make love?

Thha. Thump! Thha-Thump!
Should we go out to dinner?
Thump! Thump!

Did you like the meal?
                    ?
These silences mean something.

But when your car turns in the driveway,
the *Thha! Thump! Thump!* makes the day
worthwhile. Turn over in the black of night

and *thump thump,* it's so easy to fall back
to sleep. The smell of an old lover's shirt
Thhha. Thump! after a long time gone.

You can't hide it. The tail speaks.
No more: does he like me or not?
No more: does she like the meal?

No more: is this the right time? Am I
the right person? You know it: *Thha! Thump!*
No more negotiations between

the Palestinians and Israelis.
You want Gaza? *Thump! Thump! Thump!*
You want sovereignty? *Thump! Thump!* It's settled.

It's so easy. Let the tail do the work.
Can I scratch your belly? *Thump! Thump!*
Let's take a walk. *Thump! Thump! Thump!*

An Ad for Luxury

Like the velvety texture of Jack Daniels
on your tongue, like the soft leather of the Lexus
on your palm, luxury is easy to get used to.

Just slide inside it, press and it takes you
where gold drips from your fingertips.

It wants you to have what it offers
like a good lover who is as silent
as the interior of your Lexus.

You only need to accelerate!
Discard who you are.
Unlock its door and be done
with the was you were.

You have the best whiskey you can buy,
a lover who loves you as you want to be loved,
all the power you'll ever crave under your foot.

Ditch the past.
Indulge.
Drive off to Palm Springs.
Sink into a hot tub.

Be like Houdini who kept the master key in his throat
and could cough it up on cue. Unlock any door!

You may slip over the center line into oncoming traffic.
It doesn't matter because the other lane is *your* lane.

Luxury never gets old.

It may taste like Wild Turkey.
It may look like a cheap second-floor flat off I-95.

Don't worry.

You get used to a pedal that won't stop accelerating,
a lover who never wants to unlove,
and a man who'll return your empties, 5 cents on a bottle.

V.

On the South Branch of the Potomac

for Carole Goldizen

I come back forty years later to this spot, miles
from the main road, on a dock by an abandoned lodge.

An oak sapling sprouts in a rain gutter. I sit,
listening to the water niggling at the rock.

The water striders press and slide across the surface,
unaware of the current pulsing over the rocks beneath them.

They are like monks living in rooms without clocks,
praying endlessly in a darkened room for light,

like osprey hovering over the lake, the thermal updrafts
holding them like kites with no strings, effortless.

The locust hum in the cottonwoods. Otherwise,
no voices. No one. A large fish cresting the water

punctuates the stillness. It's August; three days ago
my friend was buried on a hillside miles from here.

I cannot slip over memory's current like these striders.
Their dainty legs press in and out over the scrim of water.

If I stepped into its surface, I'd sink up to my waist
and be carried to one night near Blackwater Falls

where I said, "I want to write" and you listened as the water
splattered over the rim of moonlight. The river accepts any

body that slides into it and lets it go, pulling it on, taking it
to where all is wanting and waiting to be alive

before the marriage came and went, before the children
had grown, before the 50th reunion, its invitation list,

shorter now, and all the lost classmates, even before your books
went out of print, and you, my friend with a single yellow rose

in your hand before the casket closed and time as we knew it
stopped before I had touched your hand, cold, and said goodbye.

I remember the silken surface of the water and came back.
I put my foot in this river which never seems to tire, never

grows old, and would take me again gladly. Isn't that enough?

Fire Island

How often does the ferry slip against the bulkhead,
      its plank down, travelers let off?
How often does the sun strip back the dark
      and the breeze uncurl the leaves with its foggy tongue?
How often does the ocean nibble the shore, slide back, return?
How often does the man on the swing touch his toes on the sun?
How often do waves topple one into another, folding and unfolding
      and roots dive deep, pressing into sand as wisteria spill its
      purple *ahh*?
How often does the moon drift through a cloud, undressing?
How often do lovers leave this lush scene — climb the dunes,
      head to the lamp-lit town to ferry home?

Upper Room

The air was dry, the room, bare.
I had not meant to be there.
The face I knew — no, not you.
A lover, perhaps, who asked me to.

In the dark, no words, a sigh.
Deep in the corner, a life, a lie.
Here, yes. Like this? Yes. Yes.
Before the shade lifts, a last caress.

We were there, his skin on mine,
So much desire. So little time.
You first; no you. He smiled; me too.
He touched; a groan, a muffled coo.

There light was breath, there love.
The fingers, quiet; the skin, a glove.
Found. Yet here, so much lost.
Not magnanimous, our little Pentecost.

There is you, love, and me, love.
There is no in between love.
All night, all day, no slumber,
A key, a door, and something more.

What God Wanted

The stranger's knees pressed against my thigh,
jammed, as we were, in the front seats of a subway

careening down tired tracks toward the heart
of the city. A lean Hispanic man stood by us,

his hand caressing the black silk back of a woman.
The stranger faced me, his shaggy brows,

his worn wrinkled face like someone I knew.
From Haiti? He seemed to know the score.

Not mine, not where I was headed at 1 am,
to a gay bar where a virile young man would jiggle

all he had in my face and, for twenty, unhinge his G-string.
The stranger studied me. Lights flickered on and off,

the train screeched; a voice said something in French,
then, English. Someone leaving bumped against

my knee and the stranger's hand – *Pardon* – fell
on my thigh. He smiled. I smiled. The hand stayed.

I looked at it. He looked at it. He pulled it back
yet several fingers draped over my leg

and seemed like the fingers of God in the Sistine Chapel
reaching, but never quite touching Adam –

for six centuries now, the eternal *not-quite*.
Yet here the stranger's fingers found their way to my leg.

They stayed stretched out as if sensing what God wanted.
Each thump against the tracks drummed through

my body. The crease of my pants unwrinkled.
I tried to squeeze my thighs together. *No use.*

He looked at my crotch like an old prospector at his gold.
I looked down too. We admired my exaltation.

No words exchanged. Two more stops to go.
This was our moment. This was it.

He held on. I sat there. The train stopped,
opened its doors, strangers came and went.

We sat there and knew what we knew until
I stood up, hand in my pocket, and he stood

to let me slip by. I reached over with my free hand
and shook his hand. It was soft, delicate

and could, for all I knew, have been the hand of God.
I lingered on the platform. The train swept into the dark.

I waved at the stranger who was looking back,
smiling beatifically as I receded into light.

The Sweetness

From Stuart to Sugarloaf in spring, then back to Florida
in fall, mother migrates, mimicking the path of hummingbirds.
She's 96. They're but 4 or 5. Clipping along at seventy miles per hour,
four days to traverse the coast, the hummers at night, the Volvo by day,
they make it, stopping at eat, to sleep, 300 miles a day.

Joyas voladoras — "flying jewels" the Spanish call them.
Their wings, whirring hundreds beats per second,
fracture the air with a *friffing* sound like a card caught in a bicycle spoke.

They lick sweetness to quicken their heart. The size of a ping-pong ball,
lighting every ten minutes, they arrive at her window.
She pours pure sugar water into feeders each day, twice a day.
They sip. She reads mysteries. She wants to know who did it,
whose heart beats one thousand beats per minute?

She watches her hummers watch her. She fetches flowers.
But she'll be back. The feeders are filled. She traipses in
the fresh mountain air. The first ripe raspberries, the tartness
on her tongue. High bush blueberries, succulent, in her muffins.

So the summer goes. The bright blare of lilies
with their luscious nectar, the ruddy curl of bee balm,
the delicate halo of impatiens — their sweetness, ageless
as honey on the tongue. This land, this leaf, this air stirring
and my mother, 96, sitting there, watching them dart and drink
with blinding wings, her book opened like a heart.

Come on, listen, this will not last.

When

3 am   you will wake
a crevasse of light   that's all

from your room
your feet creep down the stairs

daily meditations
aroma of coffee
black of morning

when I wake   hours later
the driveway   this December morning
will be shoveled
there will be   quiet
one light in the dining room

you're gone to the gym
the tracks from your car
covered already

rooms eerily empty

bunny   in his cage
nestled in shredded newspaper
with news   from summer   last
his large eyes alert
for lettuce

on the side table
a cup of coffee   one sip left
as if it's expecting you'll be back

you will come back
while I'm in the shower
will cut the grapefruit and an apple
fit them in a bowl together   snug

when I come down the stairs
I'll see you in the lounge chair reading

Good morning you say
before I know it   it is

Still Life

2 black shoes in the hall,
shucked

one
                askew
its tongue out

        like an old dog panting;

the other upright,
        eyes open,
                        attentive,

both worn,
        yet buffed —

        as you do
                polish caked on Kleenex
                the   brush
                a soft   cloth

        back and forth over leather —
until it smiles

        an assurance

                you're here.

Featured Speaker

Asked to speak about black poetry,
I yank out my favorite poets and drive
54 miles through thick snow
to the Grace Memorial Senior Roundtable
in a room above Dunkin Donuts.

I snare a seat across from an ex-Marine.
I smile. He does not. The ladies, with skin as white
as the mashed potatoes and with manners
as fine as any queen, serve me a plate
with vegetables, no meat.

You don't eat meat? the Marine queries
and piles his plate with roast beef.
No, I say, *nothing with eyes. Vegan.*

Weird, he says and scrapes his knife at the beef.
The pecan pie arrives after I speak of Dunbar, Langston,
and King, his long march for voting rights.

The Marine blurts out,
Wanta know why there was no violence on that march?

What march? I put the poems down.

Selma.

So he was there. Highway 80.
'65. King's march to Montgomery.

Why? I ask, *was there no violence?*

He stands, jabs his finger at me.
I'll tell you why: because the Alabama
National Guard (and I was one) were
instructed by our esteemed governor,
Mr. George Wallace, to shoot to kill
if anyone had dared stepped out of line,
and I, for one, would have, if they had.

The ladies study him hard. I do too.
They eye us and wait for words
to shuttlecock across their greens
and potatoes. But I continue to read
Gwendolyn Brooks, her 'real cool boys'; then,
Patricia Smith's poem about Nicole, her "mother is gone,
murdered by slim silver needles and a stranger. . ."
and, last, Timothy Seibles' poem about 14-year-old
street kids who taunt some boy,
"Cat got your balls?"

The Marine takes careful aim and fires.
Hey, watch your language, boy.
He stares at me – his pecan pie, only crust –
then storms out the door.

Has he forgotten that not a single
black was registered in Lowndes Country
where Mrs. Liuzzo from Detroit
whose sons and husbands encouraged
her to, "Go for it," was murdered?
It was a country 81% black,
yet 110% of whites
were registered to vote.

My own son, adopted,
with skin dark like chocolate, is
stopped by police on our own street.
Local officers check on him
– could they see his license? –
there are complaints. He stepped
on neighbor's lawn. Maybe
he should watch his step?

I want to hate the pecan pie,
but the ladies shake my hand
and ask, *Had I notes? Copies of poems?*
They want to read them and
put them in the newspaper!

I give them up gladly and
eat every bite of my pecan pie.
I leave thinking of their frail white hands
holding Dunbar, Langston, Smith and Seibles.
I drive (not far) to where the roads are cleared
from the storm, where I can make it home.

All You'll Derive

Will I ever get used to my mother falling?

First her right wrist broken, her right hand as useless
as a spoon with no handle, and then, other falls as if someone
is shaking the ground she stands on. Each time her foot
reaches out, continents shift. Atlas, weary, on his knees,
is wobbling his load. Mother, in her tenth decade,
plods unsteadily around the lake before twilight—
the crickets she can no longer hear chirp.

So when she topples over today, it's no surprise.
I carefully set her folding chair by the 17th green
for her to watch teens finish their round.
She's pleased, "Such a beautiful day."
Then, when she turns to someone who spoke,
her chair spills her down the slope. Her face
scrapes on gravel. Her skin peels off her cheek
like tissue paper. She comes to rest by a stump,
her head next to it, blood already pooling
by her cheek, dirt in mouth, on her lips.

And what do I do? I'm not like a parent
expecting her to stand up, not thinking as I did
with my daughter, "That's what she must do:
fall so she learns to get back up."

What to say to my mother who, when I fell
off my bike and wailed, picked up the bike,
pointed, and said, "Come on, get on it.
You know how to ride." And I did.

I cannot pick her up and say, "It'll be better."
I hold her and say, "Yes, I know you're afraid, and so am I."
The earth is tossing her off, pecking at her,
nudging her off a stage she wants to be on.

So we sing little tunes, ones from her youth,
They say that's it true, it can happen
to you if you're young at heart — and hope Johnny Mercer
knew what he was saying — *If you should survive*
'til a hundred and five . . . and mosey, hand in hand,
by hummingbirds who like the Andrews Sisters
hum backup and sip the last sweetness
from her feeders, ones she fills each day.

The Skin of You

The slow withering away of you
after the white cells join the red
and hasten out of town leave

the bones of your face like a battleground
of stark ridges and gaunt ravines where
the living are already carried off for burial.

The hollow in your cranium shines
like cobalt embers where your eyes
hold their ground. I call your name.

In that moment when death looks at me
and says, "It's me, your brother,"
I want to claim, "I don't know you."

My arms fold around your bony
shoulders and ribs and hold onto
what was left of you, there in a chair,

your legs thin and stiff as the chair's.
From trellis by the back door, grapes —
ripe, ruddy — are ready. I pick clusters,

savor the bittersweet taste of flesh
and pulp. "No thanks," you say
when I offer you some. But you smile.

Finally, I recognize a face I knew.
A smile, large, robust, fills out
the shrunken skull with teeth

that seem whiter than I remember.
I smile back at it. The two of us put on
smiles we used for photographs —

two boys like ads for happiness
on Christmas cards. You reach out
and take my hand. "I'll be all right,"

you say, "just see." A grape sits
on my tongue, its skin taut,
its sweetness leaking through.

The Last Great Sermon of the Earth

These October mornings three goldfinches
light on the amaranth, its purple plume,
listening for one kind word, one cry for bells to chime
because this day, there is the last great sermon of the earth.
The psalms have already been sung. The wasp is desiccated
in his paper cell and the children do not go out to play.
Listen, it's the little voices needing to be heard — the voices
of moles who love darkly, the last wasp on the back porch preening
and wanting to enter the last great sermon of the earth.
The fruit flies suck the over-ripened berries and stick on the sill.
The banker counts out bills on the counter. They don't add up.
The book of what-comes-next is opened to the verse
about the charm of a baby's fingers in your hand.
It speaks of dolphins driven to madness by stentorian children
who believe in how high they leap into the last
great sermon of the earth.
All the little I's squint at what's new, the miracle that makes the sun
shine in the window and curl in their lap as if
it belongs to them and them alone.
Who will follow the word after the pulpit is for sale?
Yes, God, the poor may inherit the earth yet
are still hungry for seas to part.
Praise be to those that live in the is and listen to two mourning doves
coo on a wire the last great sermon of the earth.

Bruce Spang, third Poet Laureate of Portland 2011-2013, former English teacher at Scarborough High School, edited a recent anthology, <u>Passion and Pride: Poets In Support of Equality</u>. He is the author of <u>To the Promised Land Grocery</u> (Moon Pie Press 2008) as well as three other poetry collections and an anthology of high school poetry. He lives in Falmouth with his partner Myles and son Matthew. He is working on a new book about teachers to incorporate creative writing in the new standards based curriculum, <u>Putting the Art Back in Language Arts</u>. He just completed a novel titled <u>The Deception of the Thrush</u>.